KAMIKAZE

THE OKA SUICIDE FLYING BOMB

BACHEM Ba 349A "NATTER"

FZG-76 "REICHENBERG"

AF886137

By

The Aeronautical Staff of Aero Publishers, Inc.

In Cooperation With

Edward T. Maloney, Curator of The Air Museum

Scale Drawings by Uwe Feist

Aero Publishers, Inc.

329 Aviation Road Fallbrook, California

© AERO PUBLISHERS, INC.

1966

Library of Congress Catalog Card Number

66 - 19666

All rights reserved. This book, or parts thereof, must not

be reproduced without permission of the publisher.

Printed and Published in the United States of America by Aero Publishers, Inc.

THE OKA SUICIDE FLYING BOMB

By Edward T. Maloney
Curator, The Air Museum
Ontario, California

In the course of the Pacific War, the Japanese lost practically all of its warships and aircraft. They also lost two key commanders, Admiral Yamamoto and his successor Admiral Koga.

In late 1943, proposals were made by Japanese Naval Fighter Pilots for special suicide attacks against the United States Naval Forces to stem the might that was falling upon them. These men were concerned over the inferiority of Japanese Naval and Army strength and they had started to consider suicidal-crash dive tactics with their aircraft to counter growing United States Military strength.

Naval Ensign Ohta, the designer of the OKA bomb, was one of these men. Their idea was originally refused but as the war grew worse for Japan, support grew for Kamikaze Operations.

Captain Jyo, Commander of the Japanese Aircraft carrier "Chiyoda," stated after the Battle of the Philippine Sea in June 1944, "No longer can we hope to sink the numerically superior enemy carriers through ordinary attack methods. I urge the use of special attack units to crash dive their aircraft and I ask to be placed in command of them."

The "Chiyoda" was later sunk and so the honor to command the Special Attack Group (Kamikaze Corps) fell upon Admiral Takijiro Ohnishi. In October 1944, he took command of the Japanese First Air Fleet in the Philippines. The first organized Kamikaze operations began with volunteers from the 201st Japanese Naval Air Group. This unit was based at Clark Field, 50 miles north of Manila, Philippine Is. The first attacks were made with conventional Zero Fighter Aircraft with 500 Kilogram bombs attached below the aircraft. When the special suicide attacks began in the Philippine Islands, there was for Okinawa another sort of Kamikaze aircraft whose origin lay in events of the preceding year.

Many of the Japanese Admirals on the General Staff did not believe the time for such extreme tactics for Kamikaze was at hand. When the Marianas Islands fell, one after the other and each defeat became increasingly worse for Japan, Kamikaze attack plans were put into effect as the only solution.

During the summer of 1944, a Japanese Naval Officer Ensign Mitsuo Ota was given permission to draw up plans for a special Kamikaze attack aircraft. Ensign Ota was a Naval Aircraft Transport pilot with little engineering background; however, he applied for and received assistance from the aviation research department of Tokyo University. When the drawings were completed, they were submitted to Yokosuku Naval Depot for approval. The Navy Command approved Ota's design in late 1944 and this aircraft was afterward named "OKA" which is "Cherry Blossom" in Japanese.

The OKA was kept very secret, even within high naval circles. Japanese Captain Motoharu Okamura was given command to train the elite pilots of the "OKA Bomb." His attack base was located at Kamiike Air Base just northeast of Tokyo.

The OKA Bomb was a small wooden and metal constructed aircraft. It had room for one pilot and the nose warhead contained 2645 pounds of explosives. The OKA was usually carried under the belly of a twin engine "Betty" Bomber, although other types of twin engine Japanese bombers could be used with modifications. It was attached and partially hung in the bomb bay by one mounting lug and slings fastened under the wing and empennage.

The OKA was generally launched 25-50 miles from target. Its range was determined by the altitude at which it could be released. As air-to-air fighting progressed, two additional rocket motors were fitted, one under each wing, to enable the OKA to pull away from prowling Navy Hellcat Fighters. These rocket units could be fixed singly or simultaneously at the Kamikaze pilot's discretion. The OKA had a conventional pilot stick and rudder bar arrangement.

The pilot had at his disposal a selector switch for firing the propulsion rocket charges, a pull type arming handle for the nose bomb base fuse, a compass, an altimeter, airspeed indicator, rocket temp. gauge and an inclinometer. All control surfaces were dynamically balanced to eliminate flutter at the high speeds the OKA operated.

The nose warhead had five fuses, one in the nose and four in the base. The nose fuse was straight impact fuse and was vane armed. Two of the base fuses were straight impact and the other two were of the "all way" type. All four of the base fuses were armed manually by the pilots from the cockpit.

A post and ring sight was mounted on the OKA for aiding the pilot in aiming the OKA at its target. There is no landing gear and the OKA was moved on a special dolly when on the ground. It had a wing span of sixteen feet and five inches and a length of twenty feet. Its loaded weight was 4,718 pounds. It had three Type 4, MK 1, Model 20 solid fuel rocket motors mounted in the tail. The prototype OKA Bomb was completed in September 1944. Flight testing began on October 23, 1944, using a number of OKAs constructed at the Yokosuka Naval Air Depot. The first prototype was a pilotless OKA 11. It was launched from a Mitsubishi G4M "Betty" Bomber, high above Sagami Bay near Tokyo, at an altitude of 13,000 feet. The test trials were successfully completed and production was increased by adding two additional plants into producing the OKA bomb: Fuji Hikok and Chigasaki-Seisakusho.

The OKA MXY-7 was built as a Training Glider for pilot training. It differed from the armed OKA 11 primarily in having no rocket powered motor or warhead. A large skid was fitted beneath the fuselage and a smaller one beneath each wing for landing. In order to simulate combat load conditions of the OKA 11, water ballast tanks were fitted at the front and rear of the cockpit. For landing the water was discharged, thereby reducing the weight considerably.

The testing of the prototype OKA MXY-7 Training Glider was carried out by a Japanese Naval Man—Pilot Officer Nagoro at Hykurigaharu Air Base. On October 31, 1944, after the test was completed, he reported the flight handling characteristics were very good. Later the water ballast tanks were deleted as being unnecessary. A total of forty-five OKA MXY-7's were built. One example can be seen today in the Air Force Museum at Dayton, Ohio; however, the skid has been removed to make it appear as an OKA 11.

The OKA pilot would ride in the mother bomber until the target area was approached. He would then climb through the bomb bay of the mother plane into the cockpit of the OKA.

When the enemy position had been made known to the pilot, he would then signal his readiness to the bomber crew. He would pull the release handle and would be on his way in his missile of destruction. Once the release handle was pulled it became a one-way trip for the pilot. American propaganda during the war stated that the Japanese pilots were locked in their cockpit. This was not true. The pilot would glide the OKA toward the remaining distance to the target area, whereupon after selecting the target would ignite all three rocket motors and crash dive into the target at over 600 miles per hour. Needless to say it was very hard to down this aircraft once the Kamikaze aircraft was in the air under its own power.

When the OKA bomb became known it was labeled as the "BAKA BOMB" or "Fool Bomb" and this name prevails to this day.

It took a little over six months to train a pilot for the OKA Special Attack Mission. These men were carefully selected from throughout the Navy Air Force and all were well qualified.

With the invasion of Okinawa, Japan knew the crushing might of the United States Navy had to be stopped. Fifty OKA 11's were selected to meet this challenge and on the first day of the Okinawa Invasion, four United States carriers were hit and damaged. The U.S.S. Enterprise, Yorktown, Intrepid, and Franklin by OKA Suicide Flying Bombs.

On March 21, 1945, United States carriers were again sighted just south of Kyushu. Japanese Admiral Ugaki, 5th Air Fleet Commander, took this opportunity for using OKA 11's from Kanoya Air Base.

Fighter aircraft protection was assigned but it was felt more fighter aircraft would be needed to protect the slow and vulnerable G4M "Betty" Bomber mother aircraft. The Japanese Navy was well aware of the capabilities of the U.S. Navy's very fine Grumman F6F "Hellcat" fighters.

The special attack group consisted of sixteen OKA and eighteen mother planes. The flight leader was Naval Commander Goro Naraka. One of the Kamikaze pilots remarked on this sortie: "We are sixteen warriors manning our aircraft. May our death be as sudden as the shattering of crystal." Only thirty Japanese fighters were available to provide fighter escort protection and with this news, the chance for success in this mission became doubtful. The attack was launched regardless and at 4 p.m. at a point sixty miles short of the sighted U.S. fleet, fifty Grumman F6F "Hellcats" attacked the OKA bomber force and destroyed the entire group before the deadly OKA bombs could be released. An actual photograph taken during this mission—showing the shooting down of an OKA and mother aircraft is shown in this book.

In November 1944, the world's largest aircraft carrier at the time, the gigantic Shinano, left Yokosuka Bay during the darkness of night to transport fifty OKA bombs to the Philippine Islands. But, as it got under way it was spotted and tracked by a U.S. Naval Submarine and sunk on November 29, 1944, off the Japanese mainland. Thus, the projected use of the OKA in the Philippines was precluded.

Special OKA groups of the 721st and 722nd squadrons were based at Kanoya, Miyazaki, Oita, Atsuki and Kamatsu Air Base. The chief targets for the OKA special attack group lay chiefly at Okinawa and the surrounding waters. Early Kamikaze pilots were replaced by new ones, who in turn were replaced by still newer pilots. Some Cherry Blossoms had fallen but there were still more to come.

The initial landings on Okinawa were met with little enemy opposition, but the fighting became fierce as U. S. forces went to the interior of the island.

One of the big surprises to U. S. Technical Air Intelligence men was the capture of six new Japanese "OKA" Bombs in caves near Kadena Airfield. These OKA bombs came as a complete surprise to U. S. forces. These special attack aircraft had only arrived from Japan a few weeks before the invasion. They were assembled and were ready for use when U. S. Naval fighters hit the airfield and destroyed their mother aircraft.

The Kamikaze Special Attack Corps derived their name after the typhoon which frustrated the Mongolian invasion of Japan in 1280.

The man who was given responsibility for the formation of the Kamikaze Corps was Vice Admiral Ohnishi. The success of his organization is attributable to the bond of feeling and purpose which existed between he and his men. The watchword of the Kamikaze was "We die for the great cause of our country." The pilots did not consider they were committing suicide but rather were only doing their job as pilots by inflicting the greatest possible damage upon the enemy.

To the Kamikaze pilot, their greatest concern seemed always to have been to make sure that they would hit the target. By comparison, their death to them was a matter of very minor importance. This can be summed up as—There is an old Japanese proverb: "Life is as the weight of a feather compared to one's duty."

The Kamikaze attacks shocked the world primarily because of their certain death—self-destruction aspects. The Kamikaze inflicted more casualties to the U.S. Fleet off the Okinawa shore than did the bloody hand-to-hand fighting to the invading troops in the long battle ashore.

The Kamikaze attacks also did tremendous damage to U. S. ships but it failed to produce the desired results which the Japanese hoped for.

It is perhaps hard for the Western mind to accept this idea—a man determined to die in order that he might destroy us in battle.

One of the earliest lessons one learns in battle is that **courage** is a very common human quality. Evidence of this can be seen from U. S. Navy Torpedo Squadron 8 at the Battle of Midway in June 1942, where all aircraft and pilots were lost save one pilot.

But there was a fundamental difference in the heroism of Japanese and U. S. flyers. The Japanese resolutely closed all avenues of hope and escape; the American never did. To the Western mind there must always be that last slim chance of survival, that, though a lot of other men may die, you yourself, somehow, someway, will make it back.

WE WISH TO ACKNOWLEDGE THE PHOTOGRAPHIC ASSISTANCE OF:

TOM PIEDIMONTE
HEYEDA ANDO
U.S. NAVY
HEINZ NOWARRA
U.S. AIR FORCE
SMITHSONIAN INSTITUTE
AIR FORCE MUSEUM
ONTARIO AIR MUSEUM ARCHIVES
CLAY JANSSON

Japanese Oka 11 diving under heavy anti-aircraft fire into the target, in this case an Aircraft carrier.

OKA-11

Ontario Air Museum's OKA-11 mounted on portable dolly for mobile display. The insignia on the nose is that of the Cherry Blossom unit of the Kamikaze Corps.

Japanese OKA-11 c/n 1020 captured intact at Kadena Airfield, Okinawa, April 1945.

Rear quarter view of OKA-11 with canopy open. Note red line running down center of fuselage. Gun ring and post sight for easy target sighting by pilot.

Rear view of OKA-11 on portable dolly shows small compact size of suicide bomb. Note three pocket nozzles protruding from tail cone.

OKA Sq. No. 1-18 on exhibit alongside captured KI-61 Tony at base headquarters, Okinawa, April 1945. Note release hook in front of windshield where OKA was attached to parent aircraft.

Rear quarter view of OKA-11. The term "Baka Bomb" was given by allied code men meaning Foolish Bomb.

OKA-11 Sq. No. 1-18 on display in front of base headquarters, Okinawa. The curious G.I.'s on Okinawa got their first glance at the Baka Bomb here.

Unusual head-on view of the deadly OKA Bomb. This one, seen mounted on a pole, is on display in Japan today.

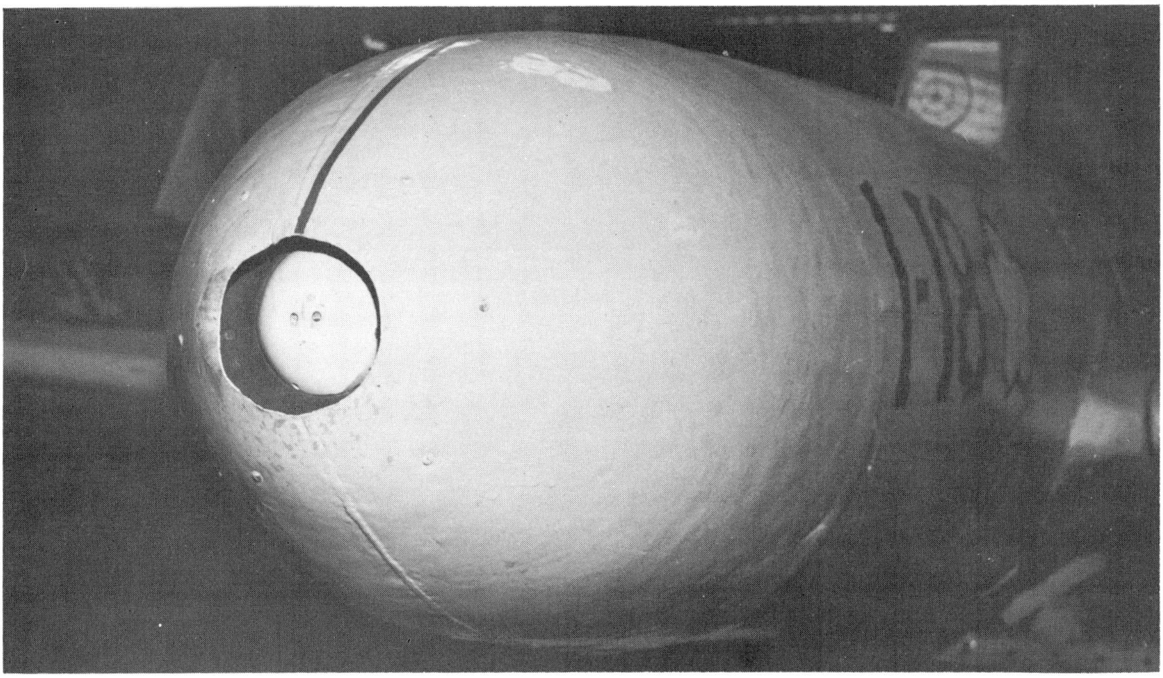

Visitor to Ontario Air Museum views cockpit of OKA Bomb.

Warhead of OKA Bomb contained 2645 pounds of explosives and five fuses.

Kamikaze pilot's view forward — showing ring and post sight.

Canopy enclosure on OKA Bomb gave excellent visibility in all directions. The canopies were not locked, as has been reported during World War II.

OKA-11 with canopy open, showing instrument panel. Note two air scoop inlets rear of canopy, one on each side. Used to force air into tail cone to carry away rocket gases.

Ontario Air Museum director Edward Maloney in pilot's cockpit of OKA Bomb. Japanese cock-pit was rather small for average American.

OKA-11 canopy. Ring sight mounted in front of pilot's windscreen to aid his sighting target. Note crude rivet pattern for one-way-trip suicide craft.

Close-up view of clean, neat lines of OKA canopy gave excellent visibility to pilot in all directions.

Rear view of pilot's enclosure, showing simple, well-designed canopy.

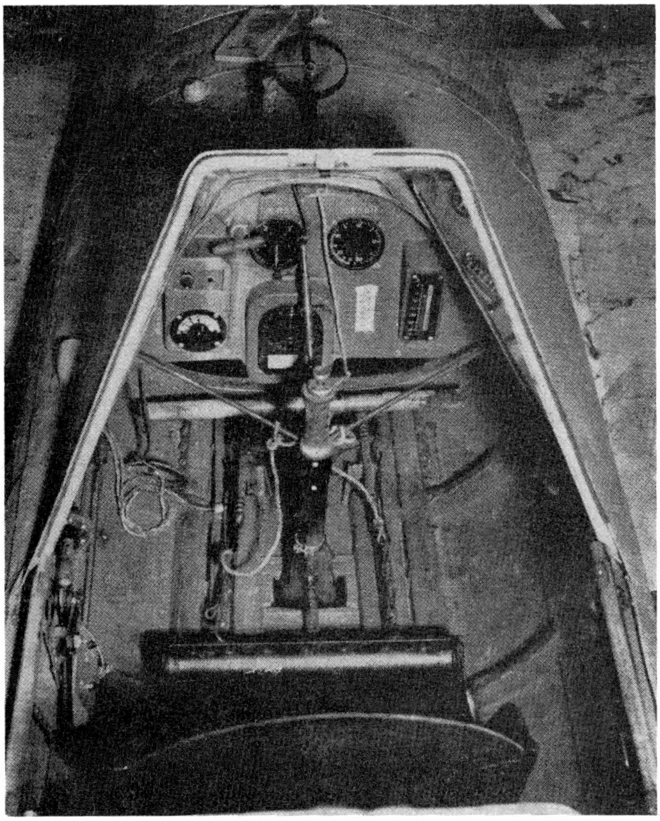

Kamikaze pilot's cockpit was simple, but well designed.

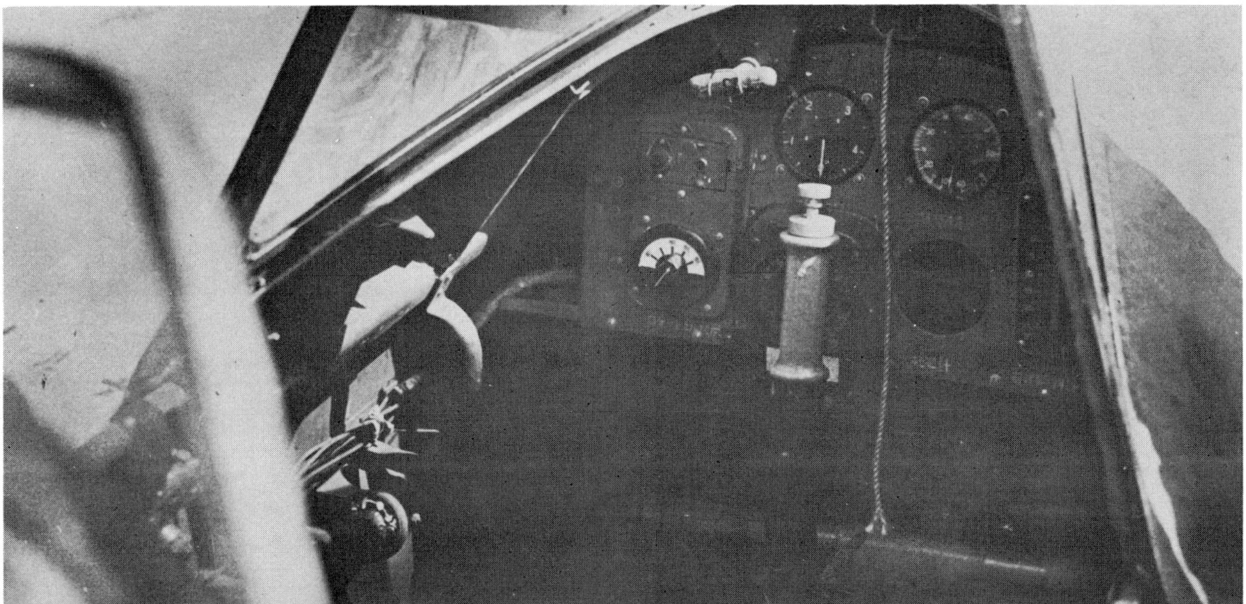

Stick and rudder bar gave excellent control. On lower left side of panel was the rocket selector switch; mounted above was the pull-type bomb arming handle. Other instruments used were compass, altimeter, airspeed indicator, temperature gauge and inclinometer.

A Kamikaze OKA Bomb as removed from camouflaged cave on portable dolly and prepared for sortie.

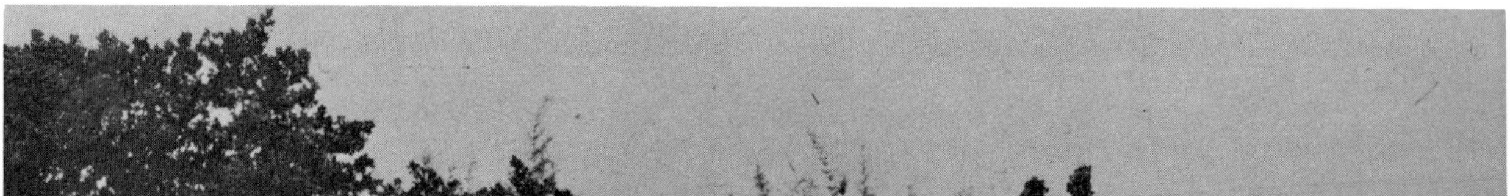

Direct rear view of captured OKA Bomb on Okinawa. These human missiles are being dismantled for shipment to United States. Note wires above OKA Bombs held clever foliage screens to camouflage area.

OKA-22

Dimensions:
Span: 13 ft. 5 in.
Length: 21 ft. 8 in.
Wing Area: 43 sq. ft.
Engine: TSU-11.
Warhead: 1,320 lbs.
Weight: Empty—1,200 lbs.
Normal—3,750 lbs.
Max. Speed: 264 M.P.H. @ S.L.
Dive Speed: 600 M.P.H.
Range: 630 miles.

OKA-22 was a newer, faster, and more maneuverable jet powered Kamikaze aircraft. It was to have been air launched by the Yokosuka PIYI "Francis" Bomber.

Uwe Feist

BACHEM Ba 349A "NATTER"

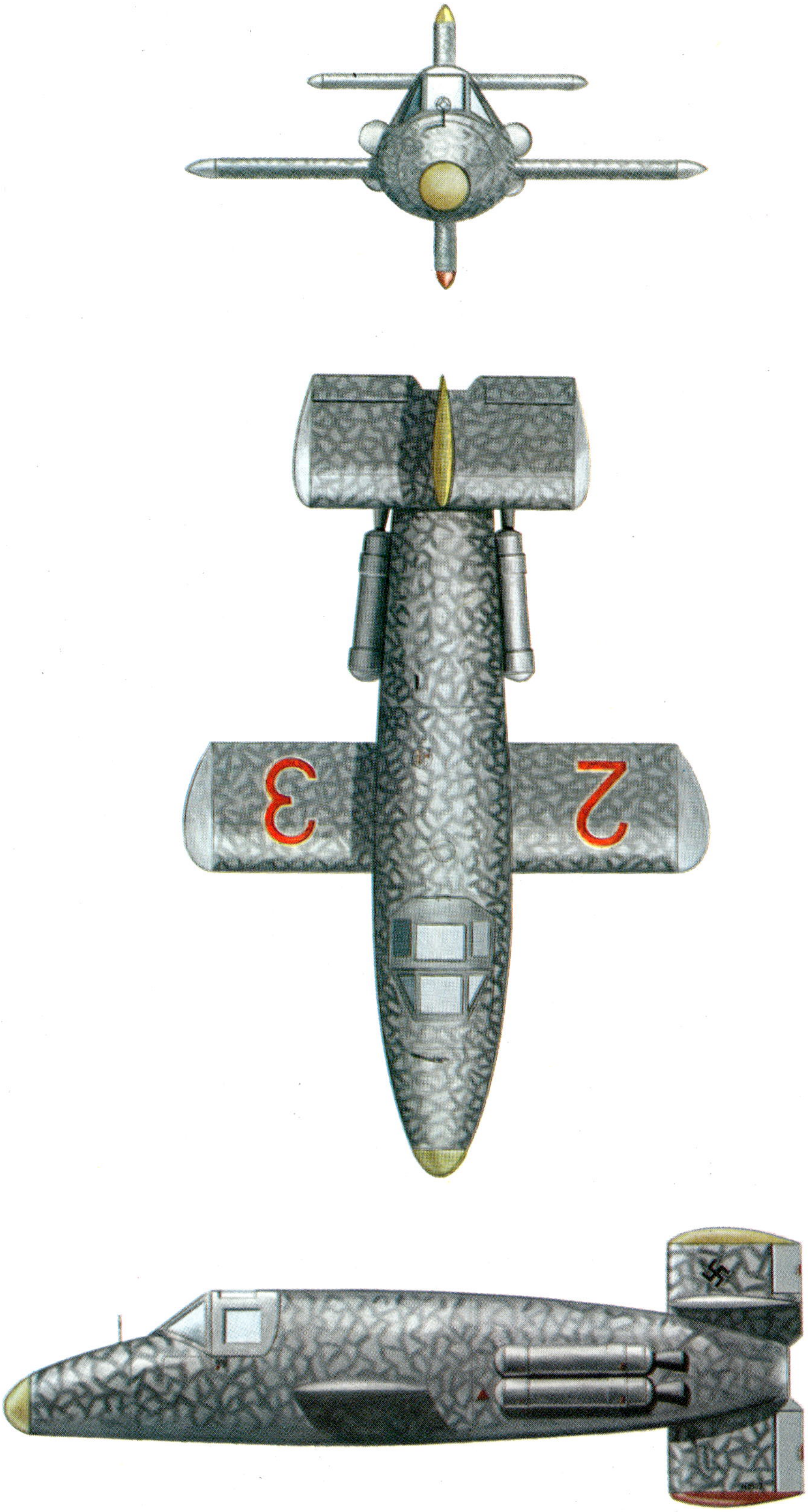

Uwe Feist

Bachem Ba 349A "Natter" or "Viper." A fast-climbing target defense interceptor. These piloted aircraft were to have been shot aloft into the bomber stream, where 24 R4M rocket missiles in nose were to be fired into B-17 and B-24 formations.

FZG-76 "REICHENBERG"

Uwe Feist

The FZG-76 Reichenberg was the piloted version of the FI-103. Developed in great secrecy for use by a volunteer Luftwaffe suicide group, the project was dropped upon orders from Hitler.

BACHEM Ba 349B "NATTER"

Bachem Ba 349B was an Eleventh Hour target defense interceptor.

FUJI OKA-11

OKA-11 suicide flying bomb of the Cherry Blossom Kamikaze unit.

KAWANISHI BAIKA

Kawanishi "Baika" special attack bomb designed to repulse U.S. Navy Invasion Fleet.

Uwe Feist

OKA BOMB KAMIKAZES

The United States Navy aircraft carrier U.S.S. Bunker Hill is hit by two Kamikazes in 30 seconds on May 11, 1945. In 1281, Kublai Khan sent a mighty armada to invade Japan. Success was all but assured when a giant typhoon destroyed his ships off the Japanese coast. The Japanese people credited their salvation of the empire to Kamikaze — the Divine Wind. In early 1945, after overwhelming American victories on Land, Sea and Air in the Pacific. The Japanese home islands felt the crushing military might of the United States. Once again, it seemed that only a miracle would turn the tide in Japan's favor. The Special Attack Force was formed. Each member of this unit was expected to sacrifice himself, with his plane, in an attack on an enemy carrier. It was inevitable that this suicide squadron should be named after its predecessor — the Kamikaze.

The U.S.S. Bunker Hill a few minutes later, after being hit by two Kamikazes at 25°44′ N, 129°28′ E. The U.S.S. Bunker Hill was severely crippled after two direct hits from Kamikazes. It had been Admiral Marc Mitscher's flagship. 402 men were killed, 264 were wounded and the veteran carrier was put out of action for the rest of the Pacific war.

The U.S.S. Franklin was hit South East of the Japanese home island of Kyushu on March 19, 1945. Navy men rush forward to put out fires.

The U.S.S. Franklin lists 15 degrees to port while crewmen topside survey the damage. The cruiser U.S.S. Santa Fe stood by the Franklin to assist the stricken carrier.

DESTRUCTION OF AN OKA BOMB

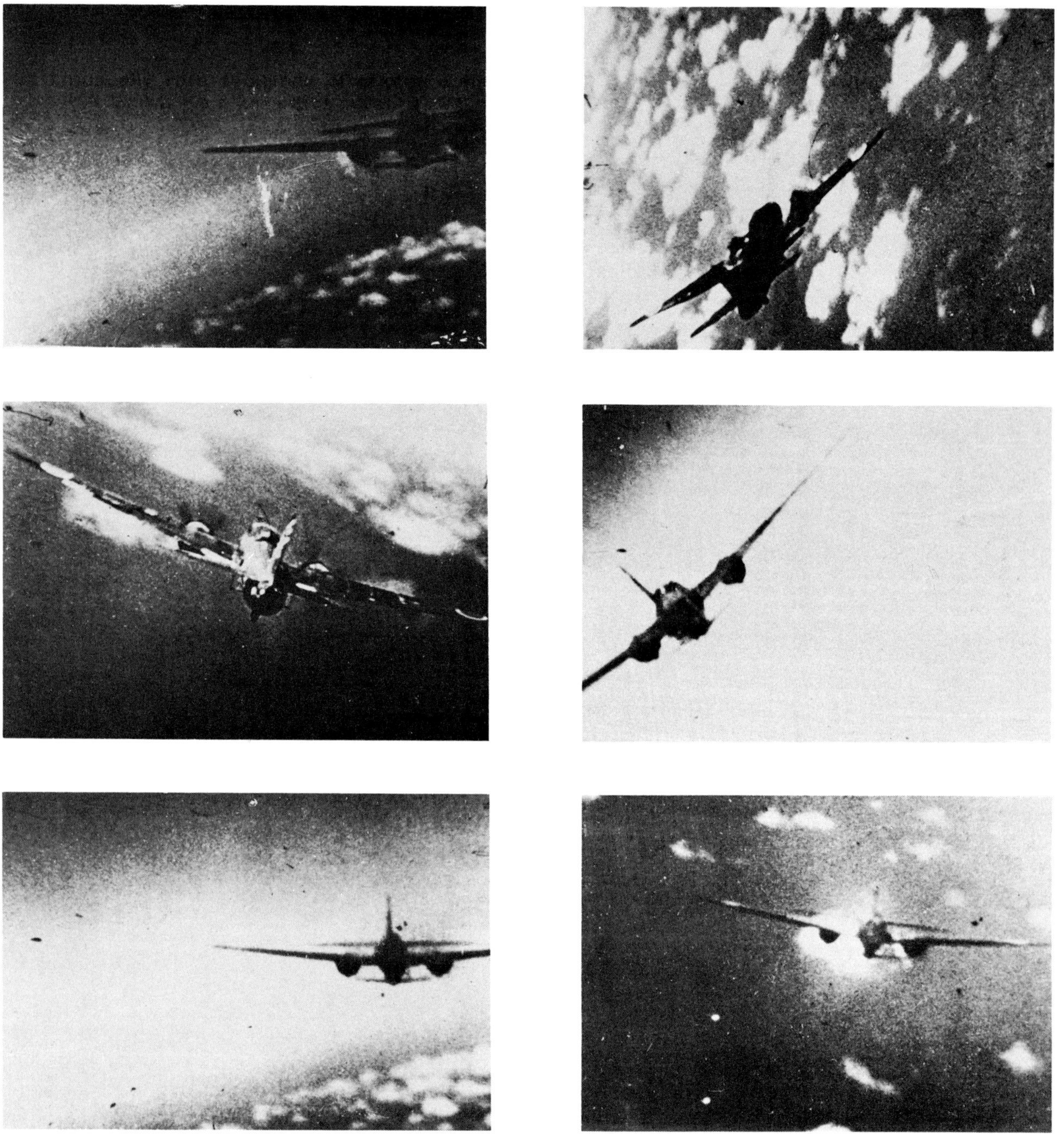

Unusually rare sequence of photographs showing the sighting and final destruction of an OKA Bomb Kamikaze and parent G4M "Betty" aircraft.

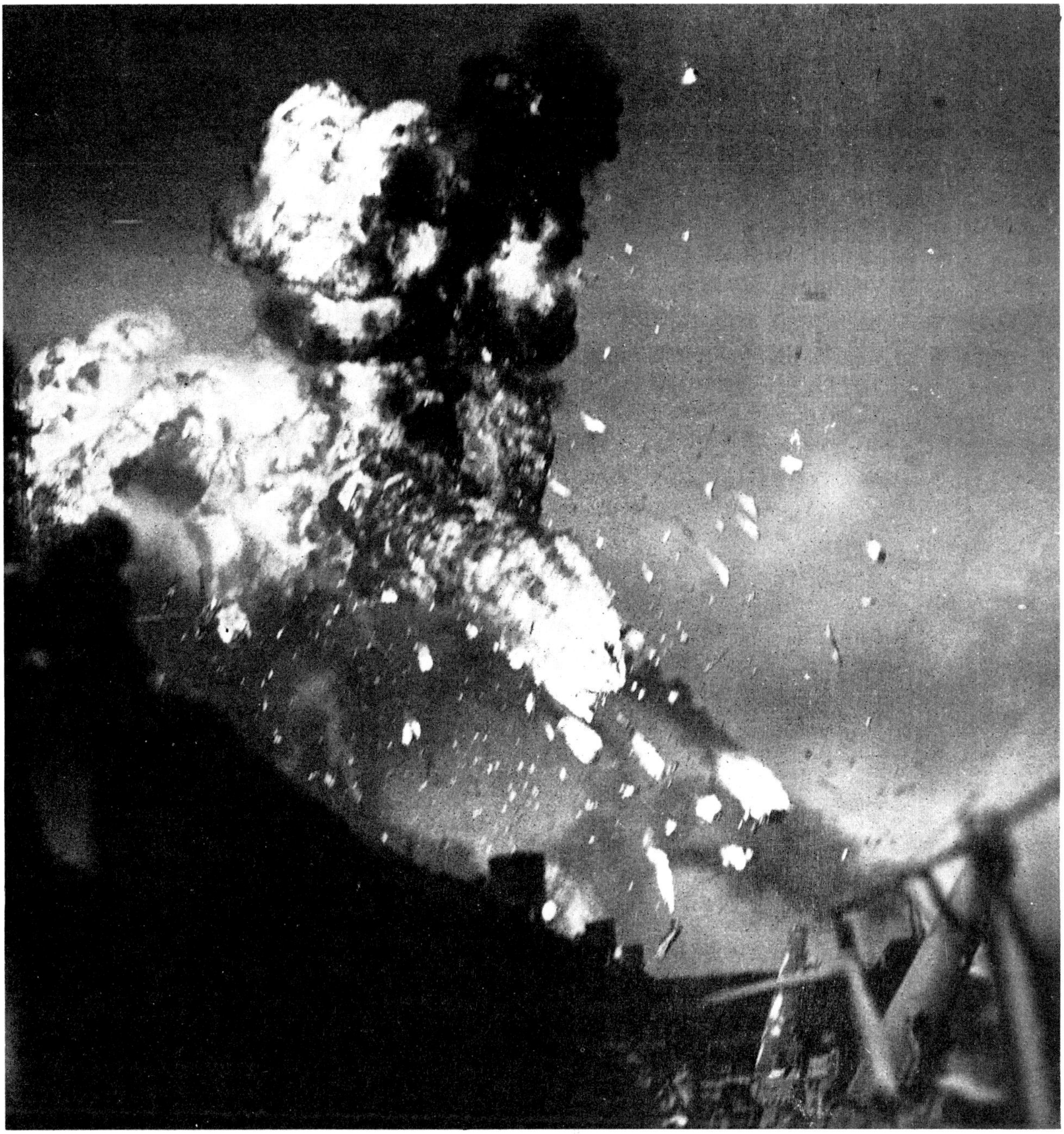

Impact of Japanese Kamikaze on the flight deck of the aircraft carrier U. S. S. Intrepid, November 25, 1944. The Japanese special attack force from Mabalacat in the Philippines sortied to strike this Essex class carrier and inflict considerable damage. Kamikaze pilots were taught to make the elevators on enemy carriers the chief target. Inoperative elevators rendered a carrier ineffective for battle.

We see here a man determined to die in order that he might destroy a carrier in the process. Each Kamikaze was watched with a hypnotic fascination by crew members aboard ships of the U. S. Fleet. Men watched each plunging Kamikaze with a detached horror of one witnessing a terrible and tragic spectacle, rather than as the intended victims.

Burning fires on the carrier deck aboard the U. S. S. Intrepid are extinguished by Navy fire-fighters. The final clean-up was a messy business, for the deck is littered with debris and burning fragments from the Kamikaze plane. To the American fighting man, the Divine Wind or Kamikaze was just another form of Banzai charge, made by men experiencing the bitterness of defeat and unwilling to accept that reality of fact.

Suicide Kamikaze hits carrier deck of U.S.S. Ticonderoga off Formosa, January 21, 1945. Four Kamikazes and four escort planes were sent aloft to sortie against a mighty U.S. Task Force in the waters just east of Formosa. Of the eight attacking aircraft, seven were brought down by Navy gunners and fighters.

The Kamikaze pilots did not consider they were committing suicide, but rather were only doing their job as pilots by inflicting the greatest possible damage upon the enemy.

OKA BOMB LAUNCHING TECHNIQUE

1. Flown 50 miles from target.

2. OKA Bomb is released.

3. OKA Bomb dives to gain speed.

4. OKA glides away on mission of destruction.

Model sequence launching of OKA Bomb from parent G4M "Betty" aircraft. The only time Navy fighters could down the OKA was prior to launch. OKA Bombs were very vulnerable while attached to parent aircraft.

5. G4M "Betty"— the parent aircraft pulls away.

Mitsubishi G4M "Betty" aircraft were standard mother aircraft for OKA — Kamikaze weapon. This photo, taken in early part of Pacific War, shows its use as Navy Bomber.

Late model "Betty" 22 aircraft were modified to carry OKA Bomb hung below Bomb-bay. Betty had a maximum speed of 325 m.p.h. at 16,700 ft. Note this model used radar and also carried "window" (strips of aluminum for radar interferences).

Captured "Betty" 22 aircraft were tested by U.S. technical Air Intelligence in South West Pacific area. Betty 22 was manufactured by Mitsubishi Aircraft Co. As the Pacific War progressed, the Betty Bomber grew obsolete. Many were converted to cargo duties and when the OKA Bomb was developed the Betty was picked as the launching aircraft.

Two OKA-11 Kamikaze aircraft, 1-13 and 1-10, in cave on Okinawa, April 1945.

U.S. Army G.I.'s on Okinawa hook up captured OKA Bomb on dolly to tow to dock to prepare OKA for shipment to Wright Field.

U.S. Air Technical Team dismantle OKA Bomb 1-18 for detail analysis. Note tail cone and single rocket motor at extreme left.

One of six rocket-powered OKA Bombs discovered at Kadena Airfield, Okinawa. Note Bomb-warhead is shown after removal of nose cone.

OKA-22 — JET-POWERED SUICIDE BOMB

After World War II. OKA-22 was on display at Naval Academy, Annapolis, Maryland. N3N float trainers in background.

OKA-22 was longer than earlier OKA-11. This last remaining OKA-22 was captured intact at factory.

OKA-22 used a jet engine for power to increase endurance and range.

Rear view of OKA-22, showing details of jet engine in which turbo compressor was driven by four-cylinder inline engine of 100 h.p. built by Hitachi. Only one OKA-22 was flight tested before war's end, and this one was lost on a test flight. This model shown was the second prototype completed before the end of the war.

Japanese MXY-7 on display at Wright Field, Dayton, Ohio. This OKA trainer was towed aloft by Navy and cut loose to train Kamikaze pilots. MXY-7 OKA trainer had nose skid and wing flaps. The above OKA trainer is now on display at the Air Force Museum at Dayton, Ohio.

BACHEM BA 349A NATTER

The "NATTER" (Viper) was a fast-climbing interceptor designed to defend vital targets within Germany.

It was first conceived by Doctor Eric Bachem in August, 1944, after witnessing an American bombing raid on a major German city. He believed there ought to be a way to break up these large formations of bombers.

He returned to his factory in Wunterburg and set down the requirements for such an aircraft. It must be a simple design to produce and one built with non-essential materials. Eric Bachem had previously worked for the Fieseler Werke, makers of the famous Fieseler "Storch" observation plane of World War II. His basic idea was to launch Natter on a portable ramp launcher, close to the target in the shortest possible time. This manned rocket-powered aircraft would then climb very fast and close upon the enemy bomber formation so rapidly that evasive action was impossible. He named his brain child the "Natter," or Viper, in the hope that the deadly venom would find its way to the enemy.

Herr Bachem got the support of Himmler for his design, and construction began in earnest in September 1944. The company assigned the designation BP-20 to the Natter, but the German Air Ministry (R.L.M.) officially designated it BA-349A.

When the Natter was first designed, the normal operating height of the Army Air Force bomber stream was approximately 23,000 feet, and consequently Natter was designed to defend a conical airspace of 12 miles radius and up to 30,000 feet.

In addition to Eric Bachem, the other people involved with the Natter design were: Herr Bethbeder—former technical director of the Dornier Werke; Herr Granlow—the Walters Rocket Engine representative; and Herr Zubert—the chief test pilot, who handled the initial glide tests.

Production was intended to be dispersed throughout Germany. The design was well-suited for unskilled labor in small workshops, where little precision equipment would be required. Workmanship would be sacrificed to enable mass production. The materials used in construction were low-grade steel and wood, with the exception of the rocket motor, main wing span, and fuel tanks. It was estimated that only 1000 hours would be needed to complete a Natter rocket fighter.

Originally, three proposals were made for Natter armament—the first was the installation of twin MK-108 30 mm cannon in the nose. It was rejected because of its relatively short range and expenditure of expensive cannon. The second proposal was for the Borsig S.G. 119, a 49-barrel motor whose firing mechanism was triggered by the passing of the target across the field of a photo-electric cell.

It was rejected because of its heavy weight and high recoil, neither of which would suit it to the Natter.

The third proposal was the use of FOHN RZ-73 anti-aircraft rockets in the nose. Rejection came from high costs and low accuracy. The final choice of armament was the R4M rocket. It was produced by the DWF Company at Lubech. The main advantage in using R4M rockets was that out of the large number of rockets fired only one was needed to destroy an attacking B-17 or B-24 Bomber.

The nose contained a battery of 24 R4M rocket missiles which, when fired by the pilot, would tear into bomber formations. The pilot's cockpit was protected by armor and bullet-proof windshield. Immediately aft of the pilot, the fuel for the Walters 109-509 liquid fuel rocket engine was carried.

The Natter was designed to be launched like a rocket going to the moon. Herr Bachem designed a seventy foot vertical launching rail to send off his target defense interceptor. He thus saved a great deal of time and needless weight of a landing gear. Four booster rockets were attached to the rear fuselage to lift the Natter for the vertical take-off. These rockets enabled the Natter to attain an altitude of 35,800 feet in 60 seconds. In November, 1944, several Natter prototype models were ready for flight testing. One of the first prototypes was towed aloft by a Heinkel 111 to 18,000 feet to test the flying stability of the aircraft. Test pilot Zubert declared upon landing that all controls functioned normally and that stability was excellent but that it had a hi-sink rate. It descended to low altitude very rapidly as it weighed nearly 4000 pounds with pilot.

The first pilotless rail launching without the Walter's rocket engine installed took place December 22, 1944. Ten similar tests took place before the first pilotless launching with the primary Walters rocket engine was installed and effected. Nose tests were completely successful and the dummy pilot and rocket motor were ejected safely by parachute to the ground.

In March 1945, Lt. Siebert of the Luftwaffe was killed in the first piloted flight of the Natter. He volunteered and personally requested this first flight. Bachem wanted more time to conduct tests before risking a pilot but the R. L. M. in Berlin insisted that these piloted tests begin at once as time was short.

The Natter shot into the air and climbed to 5000 feet. It then went into a dive from which the pilot never recovered. A close examination of Lt. Siebert's body showed that he was still strapped in the cockpit. Further examination showed that the canopy had become loose and Lt. Siebert's head had been thrown back so violently from the terrific acceleration on take-off that it had broken his neck.

Despite the setback, further tests were made. A newer model was designed, the BA-349B and this model used a later Walters HWK 109-509C rocket engine with an auxiliary cruising chamber which prolonged the flight endurance to four and one-half minutes. Top speed was also increased to 620 M.P.H.

The operational plan was to launch the Natter interceptors automatically as American bombers approached the target. The pilot was in contact with the ground and had radio and radar contact and ground control would take the interceptor within a mile of the attacking bombers. The pilot would then take over control of the aircraft and maneuver to a favorable position, eject the nose cap covering the rocket missiles, fire them into the bomber stream and eject himself. Simultaneously the rear rocket engine would be dropped by parachute to be used again.

By "VE Day"— May 1945, thirty-six aircraft had been completed. The first ten were shipped to Kircheim on Teck to await American bomber formations, but the ground war had moved very rapidly and this operational field was quickly overrun by American tanks and all Natters were destroyed on the site to prevent capture. The Russians captured a BA-349 Natter which had been sent to Thuringia. It was a prototype from which production models were to have been built. However, the factory was overrun by Russian soldiers before the factory could get into operation. At least two and possibly three BA-349 Natters were brought to the United States. One is reported to have been fired aloft—pilotless at Muroc Army Base in 1946 and that it crashed near Las Vegas, Nevada; however, no substantial proof has been forthcoming to substantiate this report.

The sole remaining Natter in the United States, if not the world, is held in storage by the National Air Museum at Silver Hill, Maryland. It bore the Air Force evaluation No. T2-1011.

Span: 13 ft. 1¼ in.
Length: 20 ft. 7 in.
Wing area: 51.6 sq. ft.
Engine (1) Walters HWK 109-509A 3,750 pounds thrust.
Armament: 24 R4M rockets or two 30mm MK 108 cannon.
Weight: Loaded 4,925 pounds at take-off.
Maximum Speed: 620 M.P.H. at 16,400.
Climb to Altitude: 37,400 feet per minute.
Range/Endurance: 36 miles in 4.36 minutes at 500 M.P.H. at 9,800 feet.

Artist's conception of a Ba 349 B being launched against approaching Allied Bombers.

BACHEM Ba 349B "NATTER"

Bachem Ba 349B "Natter" in display of captured enemy equipment at the Wright Field Air Fair held in 1946. Note 24 R4M rocket missiles in nose cone and post sight.

Bachem Ba 349B, as captured by American Army troops in Southern Germany, April 1945. "Natter" is on portable dolly which was used to transport Natter on ground. Note in foreground one of rocket motors used to assist takeoff launch.

Rear view of "Natter" shows unusual configuration of this rocket-propelled target interceptor design.

Captured Ba 349B "Natter" on display by U.S. Air Force in United States. Note unusual camouflage pattern.

Bachem "Natter" with canopy hatch open to show cockpit headrest and armor details. Nose contained 24 R4M rocket projectiles. Designed for defense of vital targets, its unprecedented rate of climb enabled it to reach operational altitude of Allied Bombers in less than a minute from launching.

PRODUCTION OF THE NATTER

Bachem Ba 349B "Natters" under mass production and final assembly at Waldsee, Watemberg, Germany, in March, 1945. Note crowded conditions of workshop.

All-wood tail cone assembly in Bachem plant, ready for final assembly. Wood cabinetmakers were employed to assist production.

THE LAUNCHING

Luftwaffe volunteer test pilot gets last-minute flight instructions from Bachem company engineer. Note numbers 2 and 3 painted on upper part of wings. 1 and 4 were painted on under sides.

Luftwaffe test pilot climbs aboard experimental BA-349B Natter on launching ramp.

Luftwaffe mechanics had to climb ladder in fueling main fuel tank of Bachem "Natter." Fuel for Walter HWK 109-509 B rocket unit was housed in metal tanks mounted just behind the pilot's cockpit and comprised of "T" staff (hydrogen peroxide) and "C" staff (methonol and hydrozine hydrate).

Luftwaffe mechanics hook up electrical cables in preparation to launch "Natter" while Bachem company officials look on.

Bachem BA 349B in place on 70-ft. launching ramp and ready to be fired aloft.

Bachem "Natter" roars aloft from launching tower on test flight. The rocket motor of the aircraft was assisted by four solid fuel auxiliary rocket units mounted externally on the rear fuselage. These four units developed 1,000 lbs. thrust each for six seconds and gave an initial climb of 37,000 feet per minute.

Pilot is in trouble as "Natter" is turning on back after launch. Extreme high "G" force and acceleration broke pilot's neck and "Natter" crashed shortly afterward.

FZG-76 "REICHENBERG" — (Piloted V-1 Flying Bomb)

A new form of aerial warfare began in June 1944, when the Germans launched the first V-1 pilotless flying bombs. These explosive-laden flying bomb aircraft were launched from bases in Northern France against districts in South East England and London.

The first V-1, the German word for "Vergeltungwaffe," meaning vengeance weapon, fell on English soil in the early hours of June 13, 1944. The original German plan was to commence V-1 attacks in December, 1943, but due to heavy RAF and AAF bombing raids on the experimental V-1 research base at Peenemünde, production was delayed almost one full year. V-1 launching sites in the Pas De Calais area of France were also heavily bombed, which knocked out 75% of their effectiveness.

The famous German Aviatrix Hanna Reitsch was awarded the Iron Cross First Class for her valuable work as experimental pilot of a V-1 during its early flying tests. When these unpiloted V-1 flying bombs were launched, they were flying out of control and crashed without completing their mission. Hanna Reitsch volunteered to fly one of these V-1 weapons, provided a cockpit could be added and landing skids. A special model was made, and with this she helped solve many problems in connection with the flying controls of the V-1 by observing them in flight. It was during one of these experimental test flights that she was seriously injured when she attempted a high-speed landing. This author had the privilege of inspecting a captured piloted V-1 flying bomb at the University of California at Los Angeles in the fall of 1948. This aircraft had never been flown and was in excellent condition. It was in its original color scheme. It was painted a dark blue-gray in a flat finish over-all and was devoid of any national markings or insignias. The cockpit was sealed up, and so a close inspection of the cockpit was not possible. The pulse jet engine atop the body was neat and clearly designed. Workmanship was quite good.

It had the appearance of a standard V-1 with the addition of cockpit, ailerons, landing skids and flight instruments fitted to the standard flying bomb. It had a span of 18 ft. 9 in., length 26 ft. 3 in., maximum speed level was 540 mph. at altitude. The piloted V-1 was carried to the target by a piloted aircraft, generally a Heinkel 111 or FW-200, where the V-1 was released, and the pilot took control of the V-1 after starting the 770-lb. thrust pulse jet engine. He selected the target and set the controls and bailed out. The chances of survival were considered very small; however, many pilots volunteered. It is reported that 175 of these piloted one- and two-seat V-1's were converted at Darmesbury after initial developments by D.F.S. at Airring, Germany. Due to the failure of the flying bomb attacks on South East England, orders were issued cancelling 250 piloted V-1 bombs in December, 1944. Training schools for pilots were planned to be set up in various German gliding schools. Pilots would be trained in two-seat V-1 trainers, which would be without power plants and would be towed aloft by conventional aircraft. Volunteers were on hand and the organization for training pilots was ready when word was received in December, 1944, that Hitler declared the idea of German aviators attempting suicide missions could not be condoned and that other means had to be found to destroy Allied invasion forces. The fuselage was of all steel construction divided into six sections with built-up bulkheads.

The nose was of light alloy construction and contained 1000 lbs. of Amatol on T.N.T. plus Ammonium Nitrate, which is fairly stable to heating, is shockproof and gives considerable blast effect. The wings and tail plane were of cantilever construction and were steel covered. It had a single hollow steel tube main spar and steel ribs.

The propulsion unit was an improved Argus flap valve resonance unit or pulse jet engine, resonating at 40-50 cycles per second of 600-770 lbs. thrust.

With the ban placed upon the piloted V-1 by Hitler, no further development was initiated. Most converted models were sent to be scrapped, however a few were captured by Allied Technical Air Intelligence crews in Germany. At least one was sent to England, where it appeared at Farnborough in 1946, along with numerous captured German aircraft. Two, possibly three, were sent to the United States for inspection. When they arrived in America, one was given to the U.S. Navy and one was assigned to the Air Force at Wright Field.

Three different versions of the piloted FZG-76 were produced: The Reichenberg I was a one- or two-seat unpowered glider intended for use as a training glider for pilot training. Reichenberg II was a single-seat FZG-76 fitted with a pulse jet power plant. A skid was fitted to the lower fuselage to facilitate easy landings after the fuel was expended. The pilot made a dead stick landing to gain valuable flying experience.

Reichenberg III was the operational piloted suicide version of the V-1 weapon with a 1,870-lb. warhead of amatol in the nose warhead. Although this weapon could have been used against the Allied invasion forces in France, this suicide weapon never saw operational use.

FZG-76 "REICHENBERG" — (Piloted V-1 Flying Bomb)

Captured piloted V-1 Flying Bomb on display in Washington, D.C., 1946. Wings are removed and are lying alongside. Note unusual camouflage pattern.

Piloted V-1 Flying Bomb on display at Farnborough, England, April 1946. Dolly has been fitted to prevent damage to body. Note Warhead shape on nose.

Training version of piloted V-1 was this two-place FZG-76 R-1. Towed aloft by a Luftwaffe tow airplane and cut loose, students quickly learned the rudiments of handling the piloted V-1. Note skid below fuselage.

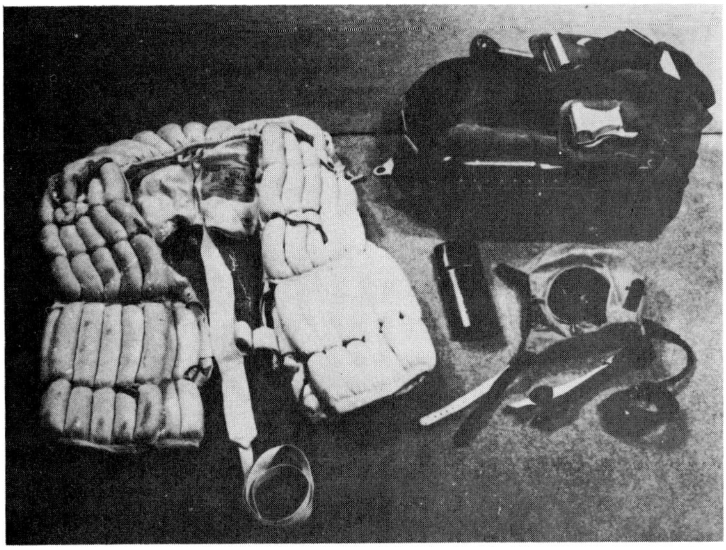

V-1 Pilot's kit consisted of parachute, helmet, and life vest. Small case contained two small flares in waterproof container.

Luftwaffe pilot in cockpit of V-1 piloted Flying Bomb. Cockpit was very crowded for pilot.

V-1 Pilot Canopy in open position. Front windscreen had 3-inch-thick bulletproof glass for pilot protection.

V-1 Flying Bomb on portable dolly is removed from underground shelter. V-1's were often camouflaged in dark green and were usually without national markings.

V-1 technicians roll V-1 "Kivic" missile to launch site on portable dolly.

V-1 ground crew prepare to hoist V-1 from dolly to ramp for launch to England. After launching bases in France were captured, V-1's were launched by Luftwaffe Heinkel III Bombers.

Piloted FZG-76 suicide Flying Bomb underway. Power was supplied by a 770-lb. thrust pulse jet engine mounted atop body.

Initial testing of V-1 at Peenemünde proved erratic flying. A pilot's cockpit and controls were fitted and Hanna Persch volunteered to fly V-1 and correct its faults. After tests were completed, the idea for a suicide-piloted V-1 weapon was proposed.

V-1 destroyed by Spitfire pilot. Plan was to pull up alongside V-1 and flip it over with wing tip so V-1 would crash before reaching London.

First V-1 fell on British soil in early part of June 1944. The above V-1 was launched from a base in Northern France and hit a factory district in London.

Original German plan was to commence V-1 attacks in December 1943, but heavy RAF raids on Peenemünde delayed this schedule.

Aero Shop

by

AL PARKER

KAMIKAZE

The aircraft featured in this volume of Aero Series will be more of a challenge to model than those previously covered, due to the fact that there are only two plastic kits available to work from. Since there are no kits on the "Natter" or the "Baika" these will have to be scratch-built. Therefore, we shall merely wish you "ROTS-A-RUCK" and go on to the Baka and V-1.

Several years ago Hawk released the "Baka" and the "V-1" as a combined 2 in 1 kit, both in 1:48 scale. These kits will be the basis for three of the aircraft featured here in Aero Series. The "Baka" (actually the OKA 11) kit is generally accurate in shape and scale, and is finely cast in dark green plastic. Panel lines and rivet detail are acceptable, and aside from a small amount of seam and joint filling, make up into a very presentable model.

To convert the OKA 11 into the OKA 22, the following modifications must be made: First, cement the fuselage halves together as usual. Now cut off the rear 1¾" of the fuslage. Note: Occassionally, when cutting a fuselage in half, I find that the line cut isn't always straight. To square up a cut line I've found that a Stanley carbide grit steel sanding blade does a very effective job. Especially if you rotate the part a quarter turn every second or third pass. Carve a new wooden tail section ⅝" longer and ⅛" higher along the spine. Mate this new section to the plastic fuselage and sand to correct the shape. Now, add two air scoops to the fuselage sides just forward of the horizontal stabilizer. (I used two supercharger air scoops from one of my son's car conversion kits.) Using the furnished canopy as a guide, carve a new canopy ¼" shorter than the original and fit it to the reshaped cockpit. This wooden die can then be used in a Vac-u-form to obtain a clear plastic canopy. Next it will be necessary to remove ⅜" from each wing tip. Don't worry about cutting into the aileron, since the OKA 22's aileron extended through to the tip. This done, you can now assemble and finish the model as usual.

The Hawk V-1 kit is of similar quality to that of the OKA and, with basic care, will build up nicely.

To produce the Fiesler Fi-103 (piloted V-1) from the kit, it will be necessary only to add a cockpit, canopy and fairing immediately ahead of the engine air intake. Using a canopy from an Aurora Wildcat kit as a guide, cut out the cockpit, carve a wooden fairing to fit behind the canopy and under the engine air intake. Fit both the canopy and the fairing to the contour of the fuselage and assemble. If your model is to be the prototype Fi-103, which was a multi-use test vehicle, you will have to add a landing skid to the bottom of the fuselage. Since there are no available details on this skid, your own interpretation will suffice.

OKA BOMB DEVELOPMENT

OKA MXY-7

A glider trainer version of the OKA 11 used to train Kamikaze pilots with this design. A large skid was fitted beneath the fuselage and a smaller one beneath each wing for landing. It had no rocket power unit. Same dimensions as OKA 11. Approximately forty-five were constructed.

OKA 11

Was developed by the Japanese Navy for special attack and was the first of the OKA type flying bombs. It was strictly a suicide weapon from the drafting board up. It was a clean design and a good appearing aircraft. The pilot had good visibility and the cockpit hood was the highest part of the aircraft being three feet ten inches.

It had three MK 1, Model 2 rocket units mounted in the tail cone plus one under each wing. The OKA 11 was first a glider and second a powered aircraft. In all, 755 OKA 11's were produced. One hundred fifty-five were built at Yokosuka by the First Naval Technical Arsenal and six hundred were built at Kasumigaura by the First Naval Air Depot.

Subcontractors for wings and tail sections were built by the Nihon Airplane Co. at Yokohoma City and the Fuji Airplane Company at Kanagawa, Japan.

OKA 22

The range of the OKA 11 was very limited and so the Japanese developed the OKA 22 to overcome these difficulties. A small jet engine was built and named the Tsu 11. It was a Campini Jet type engine in which the turbo compressor was driven by a four cylinder in-line 100 H.P. engine built by Hitachi. This enabled it to be released seventy miles from target. One rocket motor was retained and fitted beneath the fuselage in addition to the jet unit. This rocket was used in emergencies, such as interception by U.S. Navy Hellcat or Corsairs.

A newer, faster, and more maneuverable aircraft, the Navy Yokosuka P1Y1 "Francis" Bomber was selected as a new mother plane. Because of its more limited clearance, it was necessary to reduce the wing span of the OKA 22 to 13 ft. 11 in. It was longer and had a length of 22 ft. 8 in. to house the jet engine.

The warhead was reduced to 1,320 pounds. Production schedules were set. Fifty were to be built by Yokosuka and two hundred by Aichi Aircraft Co. at Nagoya, Japan. Subcontractors were included in production plan. Actual production was limited to a reported fifty aircraft which were built at Yokosuka. Aichi did not get production under way due to heavy B-29 raids. Thereafter elaborate plans were made for underground factories adjoining Yokosuka in underground tunnels assembling OKA 22's. This work was carried out even under very heavy bombing conditions and their underground factory came as a complete surprise to U. S. forces later occupying this base.

Only one OKA 22 was reported to have been flight tested in July 1945. During the prototype's first test flight the auxiliary wing rockets went off unexpectedly, just after release, causing the OKA 22 to strike the mother aircraft which jammed the controls of the OKA 22. The resulting stall and dive quickly created a situation from which the pilot never recovered. The second prototype was completed soon afterwards but the engine was delayed and it was not until the middle of August that it was completed and ready for flight. Mass production of the OKA 22 was ordered; however, the war ended before they could be used operationally and only a small number were actually made.

OKA 33

The OKA 30-40-50 series were all designed to use Japan's first Turbo Jet engine the NE-20 of 1,047 pounds thrust. They all were alike except for differences in the methods of launching.

The OKA 33 was intended to be launched from a larger Navy mother aircraft, the Nakajima G8N-1 "Rita." Neither "Betty" or "Francis" aircraft were considered as mother aircraft as they were unable to carry the greater weight planned for the OKA 33 series. This design was later abandoned in favor of OKA 43.

OKA 43

It was the final design model of the OKA type. It was redesigned by Yokosuka Naval Air Depot in cooperation with Aichi Aircraft Company. It was intended to be ground launched off a 328-foot catapult ramp. Its targets were to be U. S. Navy ships nearing the Japanese home islands. The mock-up was completed in June 1945 and large scale production was planned at the Aichi-Gifu and Oyaki factories. Construction was all metal and it had folding wings for easing storage problems. A skid was also fitted below the fuselage. To enable the aircraft to achieve better penetration, detachable wing tips were fitted, which would have been ejected during the final dive. This ground launched OKA bomb held great promise as a special attack aircraft as it did not have to rely on another aircraft in which to get it to a target.

The first OKA 43 prototype had not been completed as of the end of the war due to heavy B-29 bombings; however, one of the large catapult ramps had been built at Takeyama, just west of Yokohama and was in use to instruct OKA 43 pilots in catapult launching techniques pending production of the weapon itself.

KAWANISHI BAIKA

The "Baika" (Plum Blossom) was a special attack suicide weapon designed by two professors at the Aeronautical Institute of Tokyo in July 1945.

Professors Taichino Ogawa and Ichimo Tani share the credit for this design for the Japanese Navy special attack unit. Construction was ordered and plans were laid to produce it by numerous shadow industry plants built throughout Japan.

Power was supplied by a Maru-ka model 10 plus jet engine based along a similar German design of the V-1.

The war ended before the protoype was completed and so this interesting design never flew in anger.

The famous **JUNKERS** Ju 87 "Stuka" by Heinz J. Nowarra, will be featured in Vol. 8, depicting the Ju87B of Oberst Rudel in our color 3-view.

Vol. 9 of the "**Aero Series**" depicts Germany's most unconventional piston-engined Fighter, the **Dornier** DO 335 "Pfeil" (Arrow) compiled in collaboration with Heinz J. Nowarra and Edward T. Maloney.

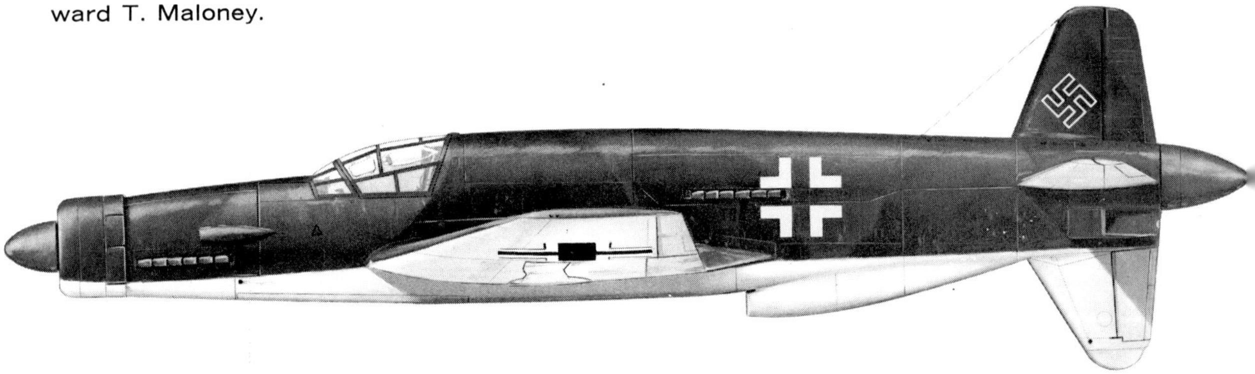